ITALIAN FANTASY

Volume 1: Without Colored Thumbnails

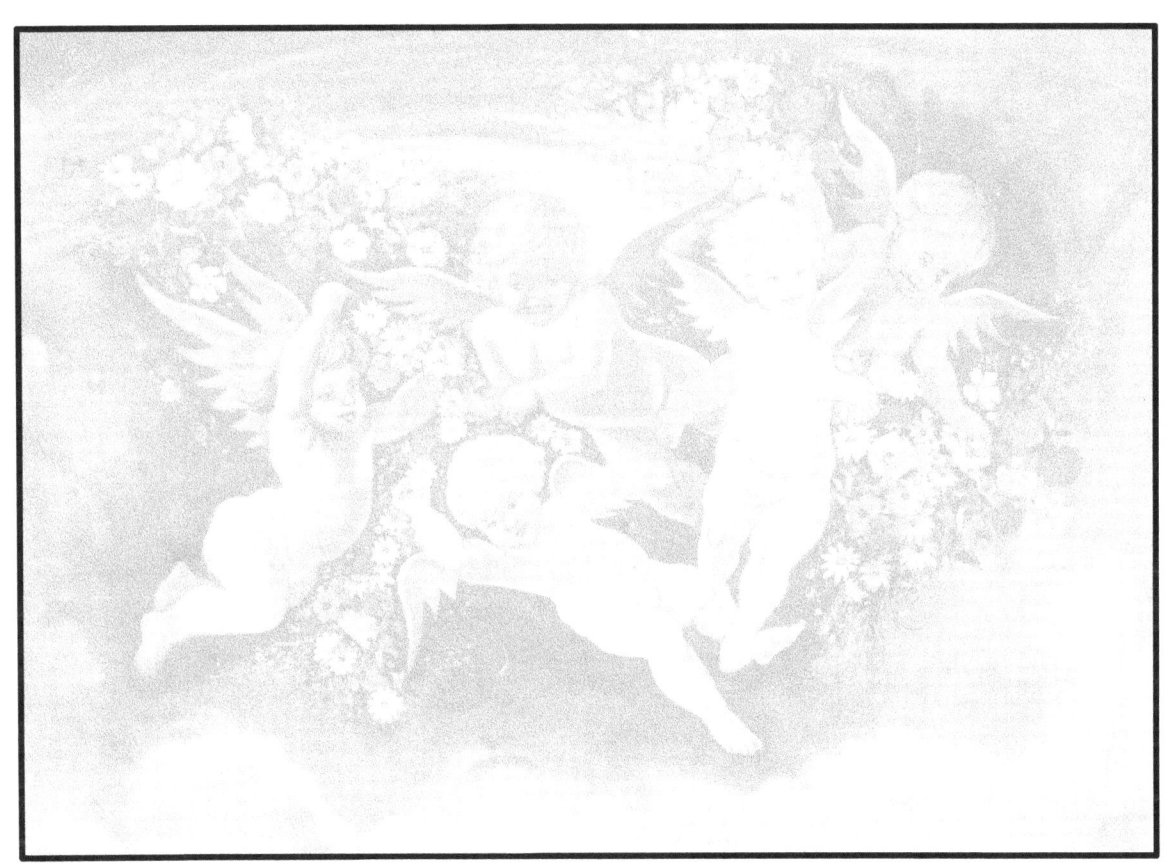

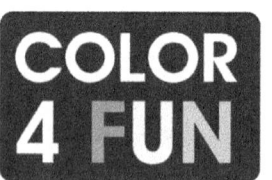

The cover for this book was designed by Pooja Bajoria, a highly-talented and dependable freelance artist. Those wishing to avail themselves of her serivces may contact her at bajoria.pooja@gmail.com. You will not be disappointed.

Dedication

This book is dedicated to my wife, Carole Jane Plaxe. Her encouragement and unflagging support have sustained my enthusiasm for the publication of coloring books.

Acknowledgments

Of course, I must begin by thanking PiRò. He has been a very dear friend for many years. He graciously and generously gave me access to his large collection of art in order to provide colorists with illustrations that are exceptionally well suited for grayscale coloring.

Also, I am deeply indebted to two talented and irrepressible colorists, Mary Hayes and Dina Nizza. I was oblivious to the popularity of grayscale coloring until they enlightened me to this opportunity. This book could not have been published without their advice and collaboration.

PiRò:
About the Artist

PiRò is an exceptionally talented and widely acclaimed Italian artist. He was born in the town of San Benedetto del Tronto, in the Region of Marche on Italy's Adriatic coast, which is where he resides today.

PiRò understands the impact of color upon the viewer's emotional state, and he strives to create brilliantly colorful art that conveys positive messages. His message is one of hope; and his goal is to impart a sense of inner peace and optimism. Fantasy and spiritualism are core elements of his art.

One critic had this to say about his art:

> "To observe the works of PiRò is like perceiving the vibrant energy of nature, and in this artist the impressionistic message continues to be told. This artist is above all a colorist who uses his access to a pallet of yellows, reds, blues and greens to create a noteworthy, cosmic movement in the style of Matisse. One can talk as well of an artistic and spiritual affinity with Chagall and Klee."

The grayscale illustrations created from his magnificent paintings offer maximum opportunity for creative expression.

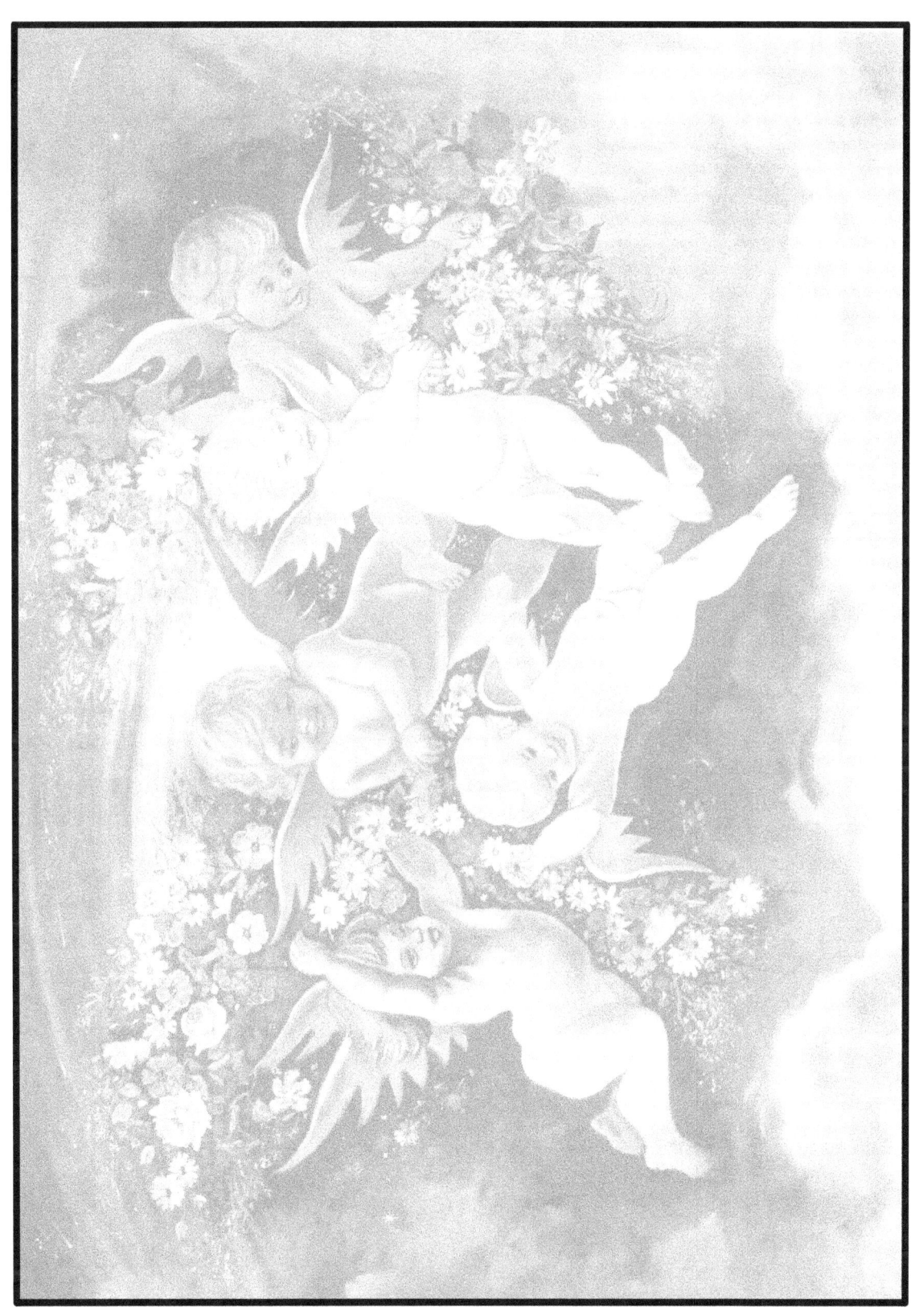

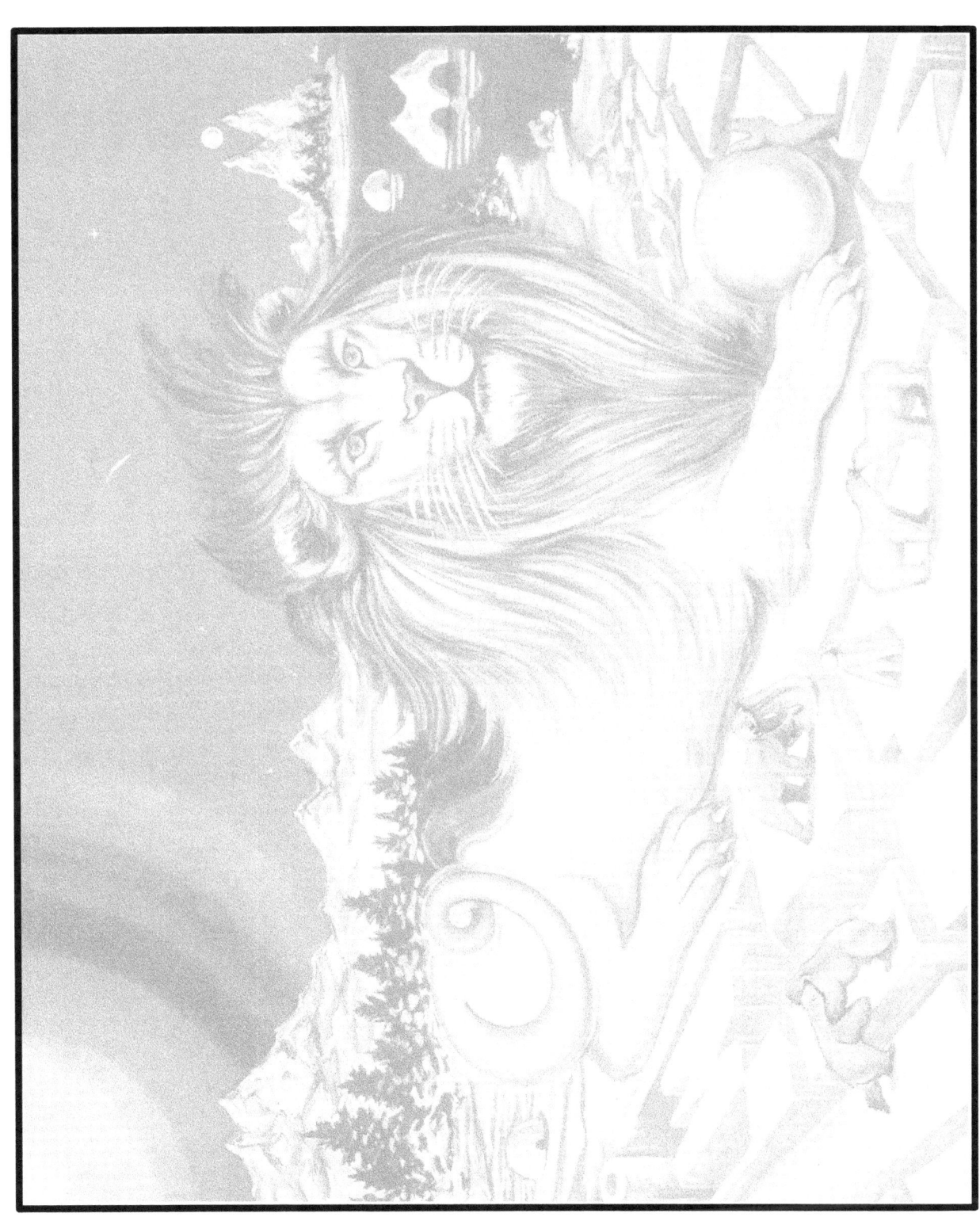

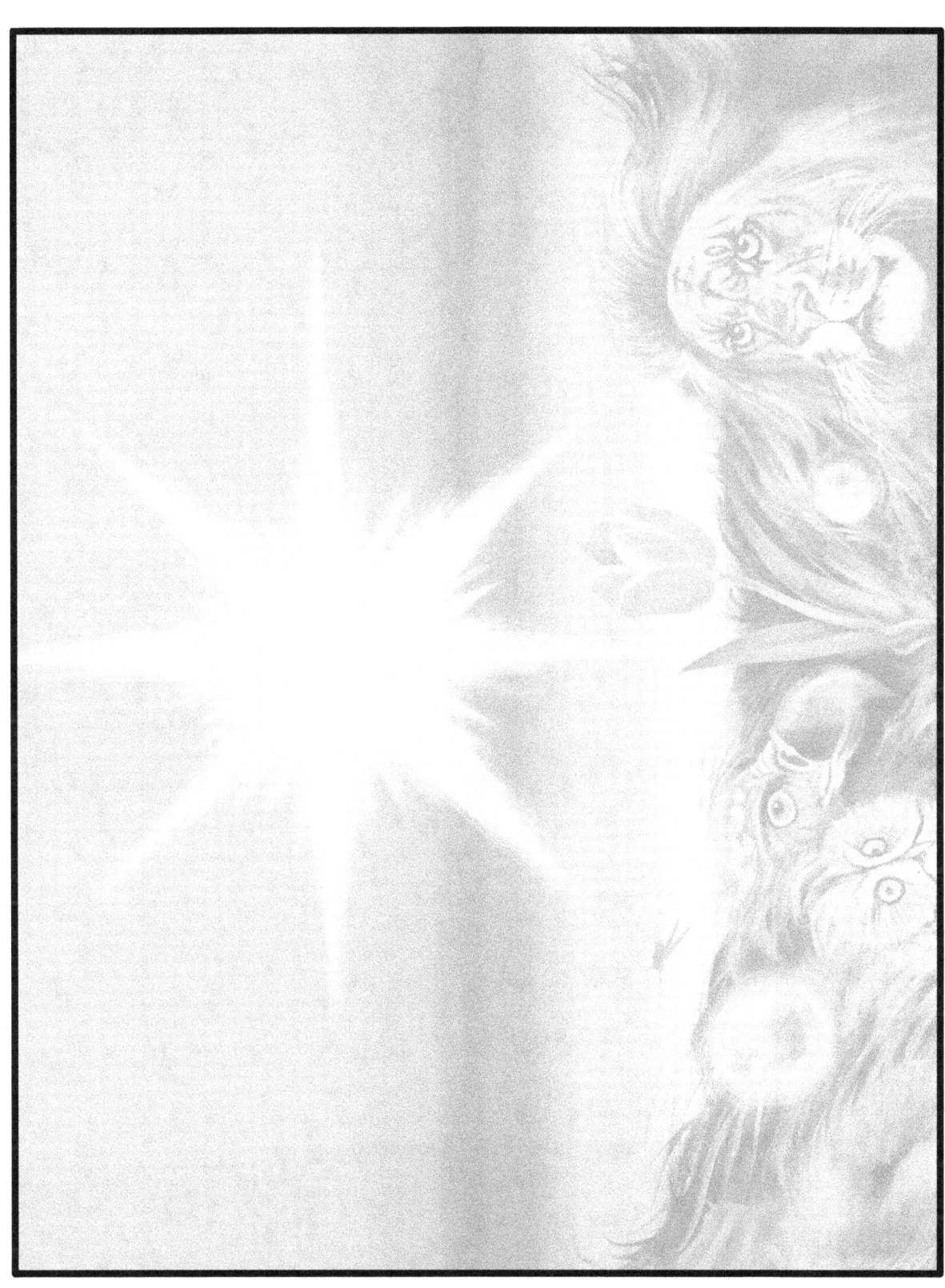

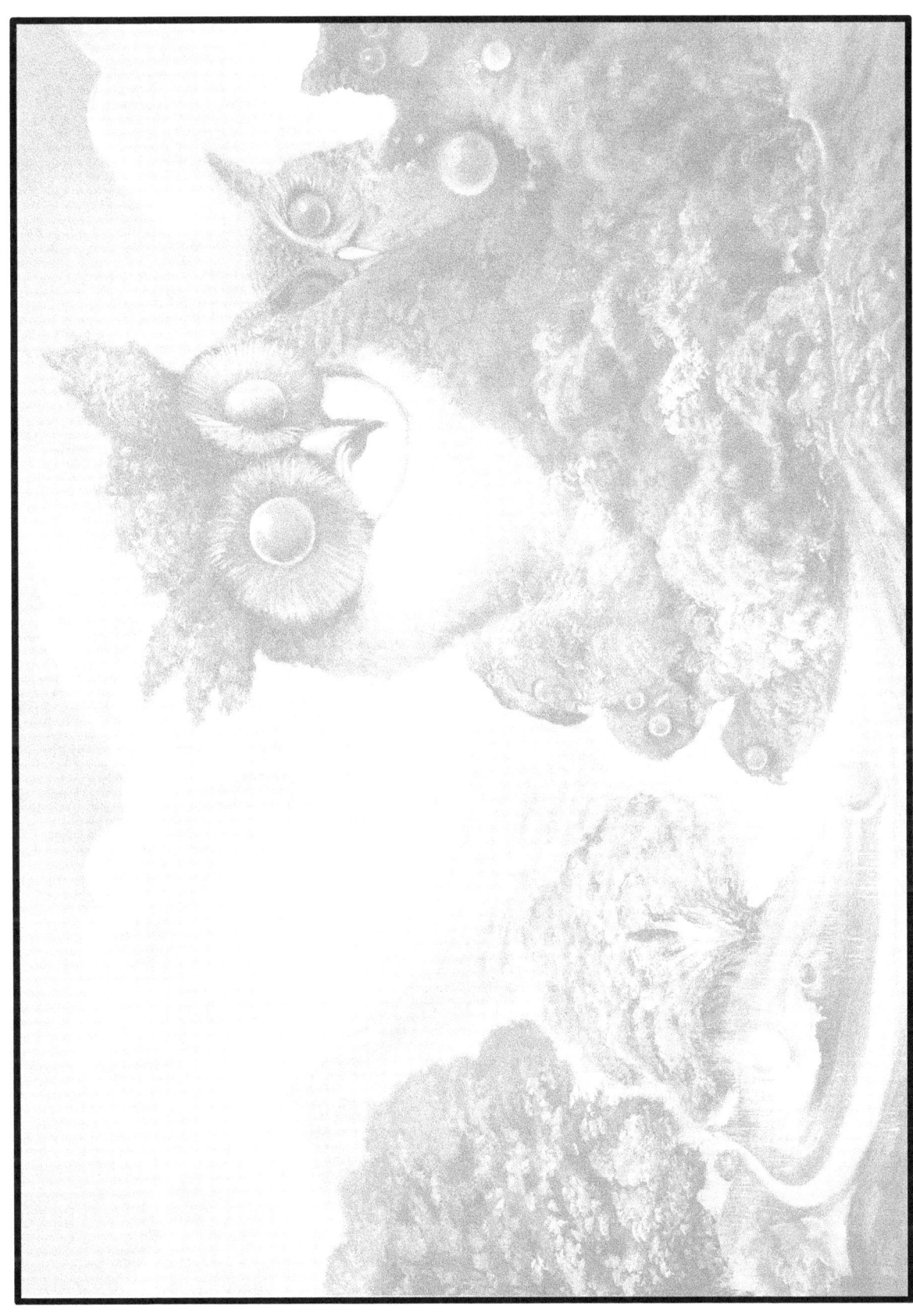

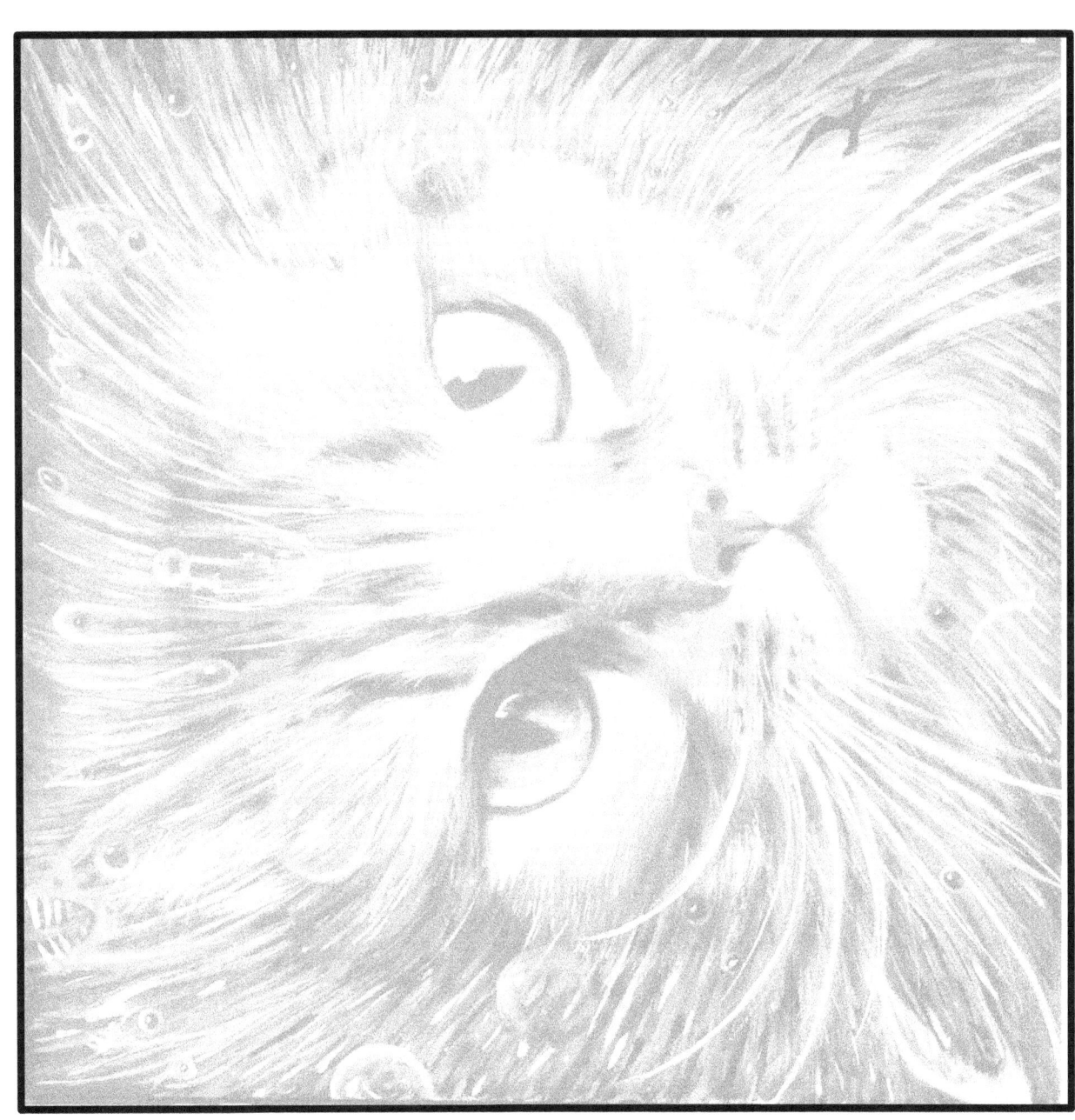

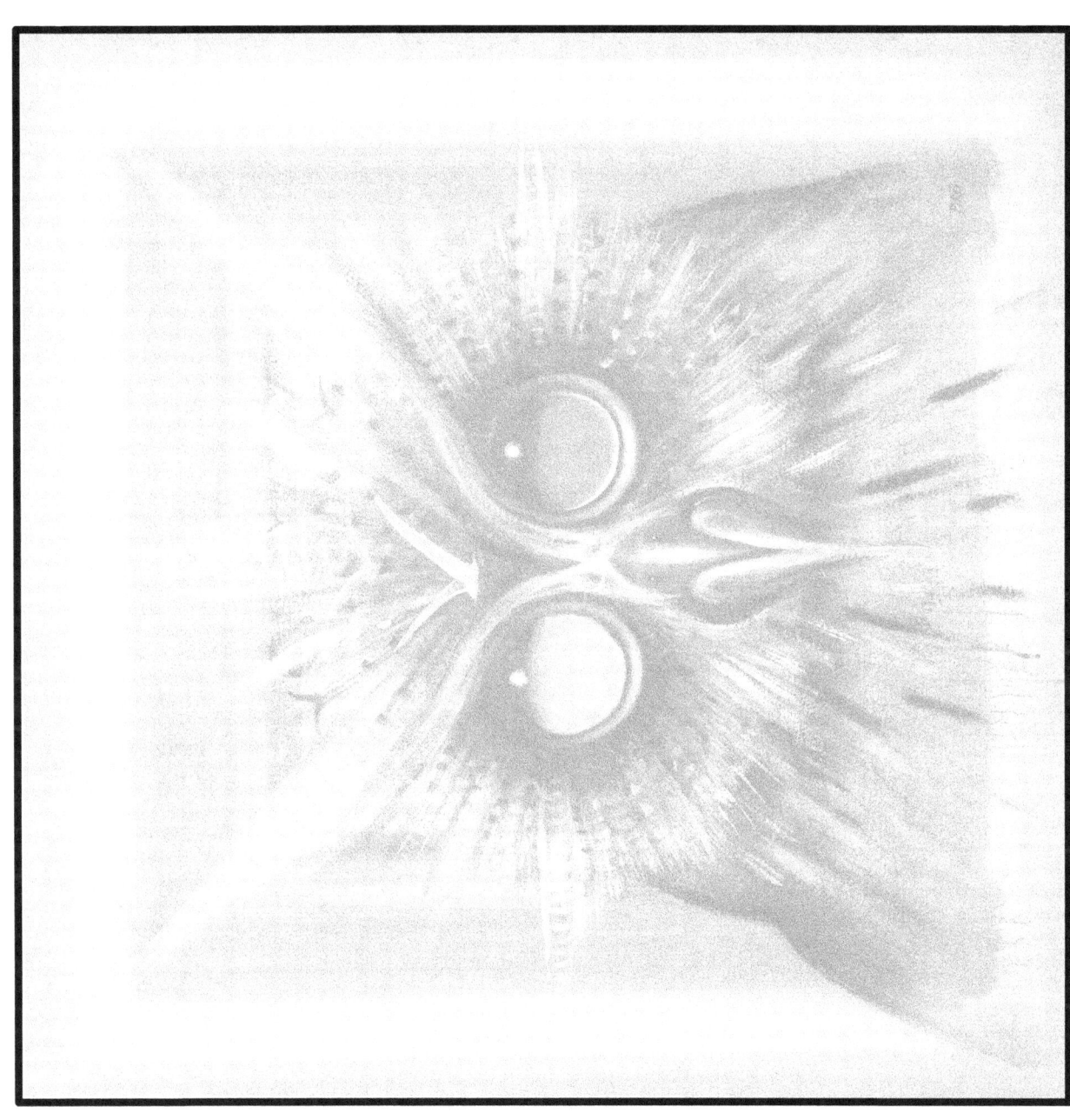

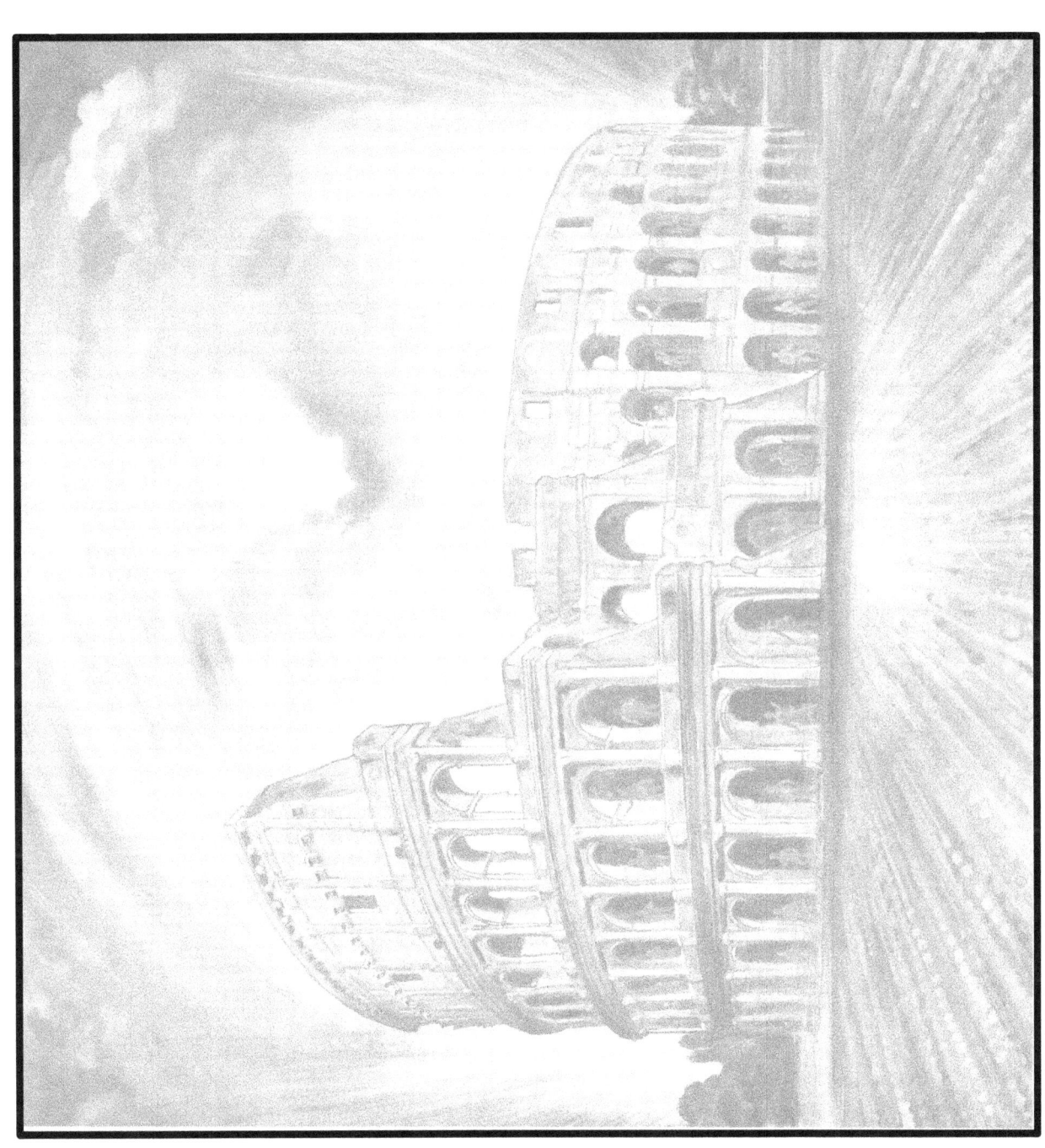

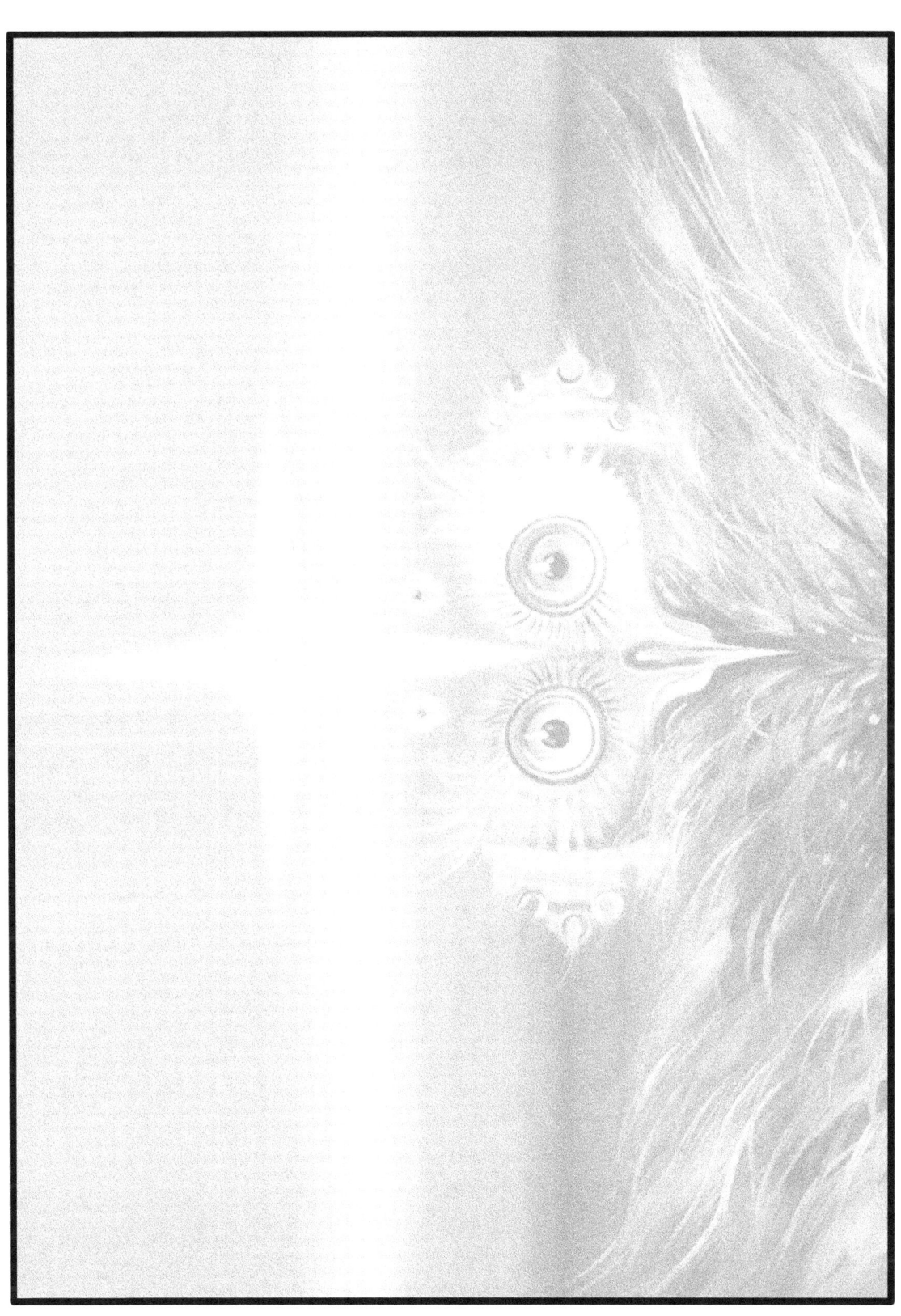

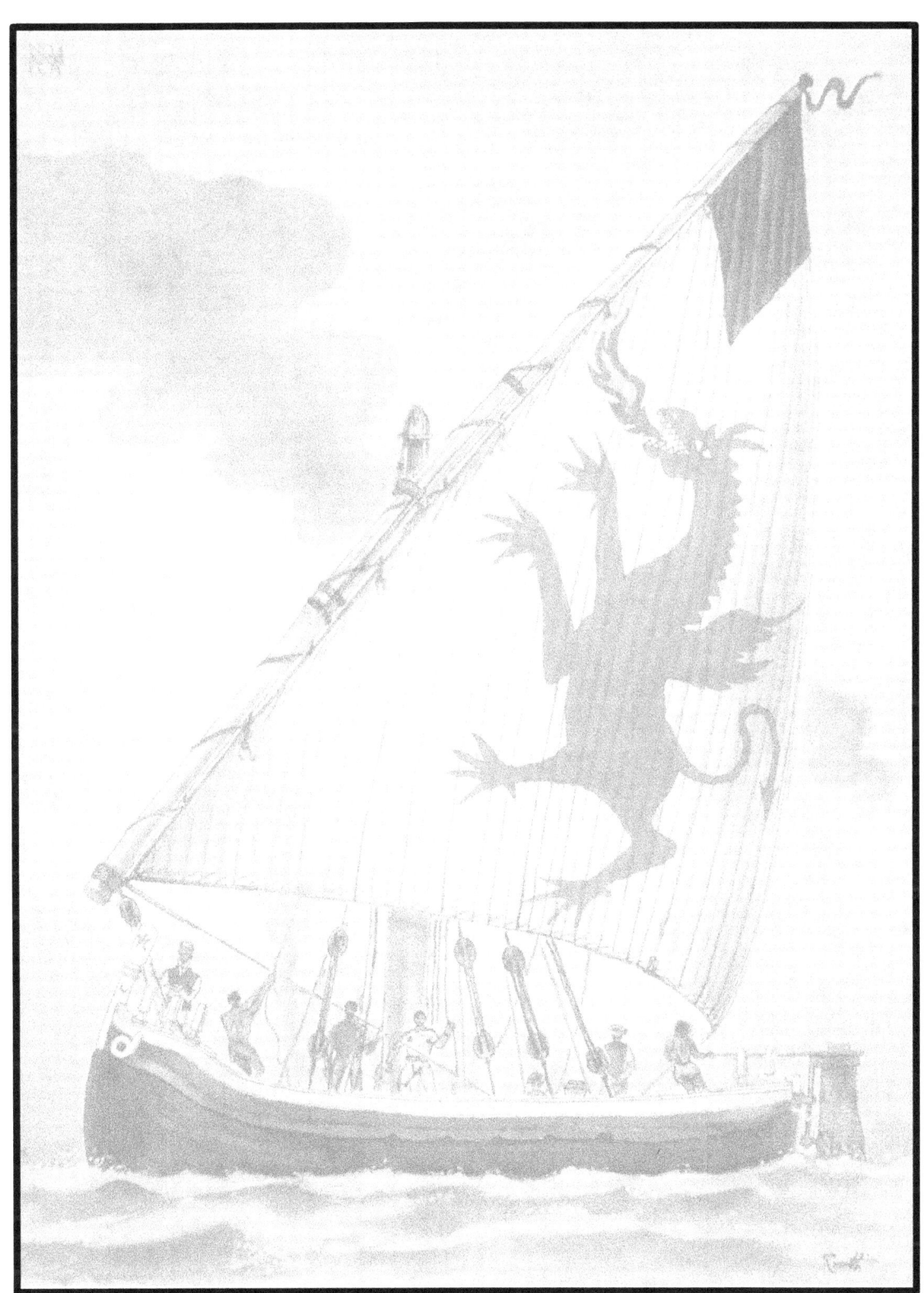

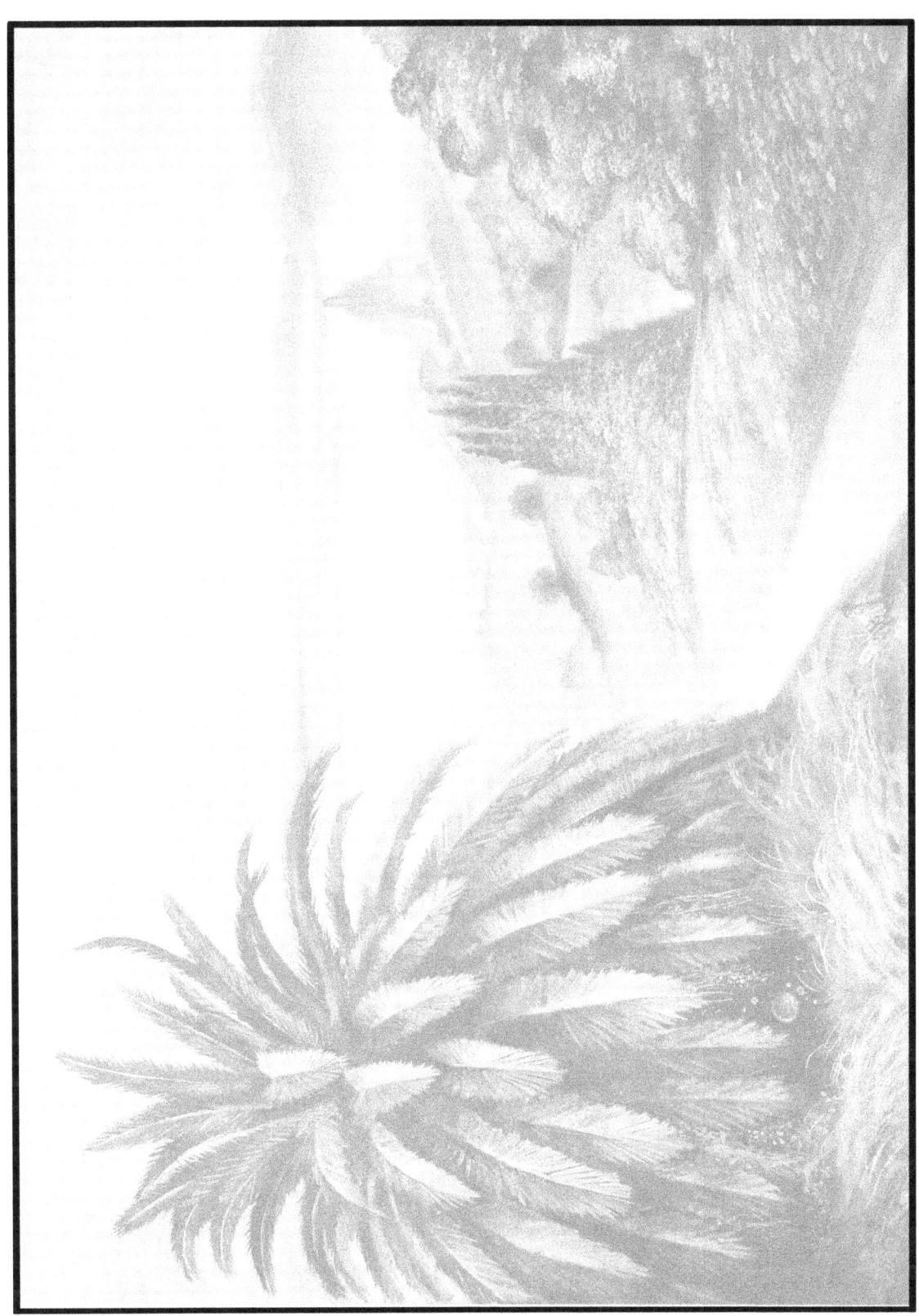

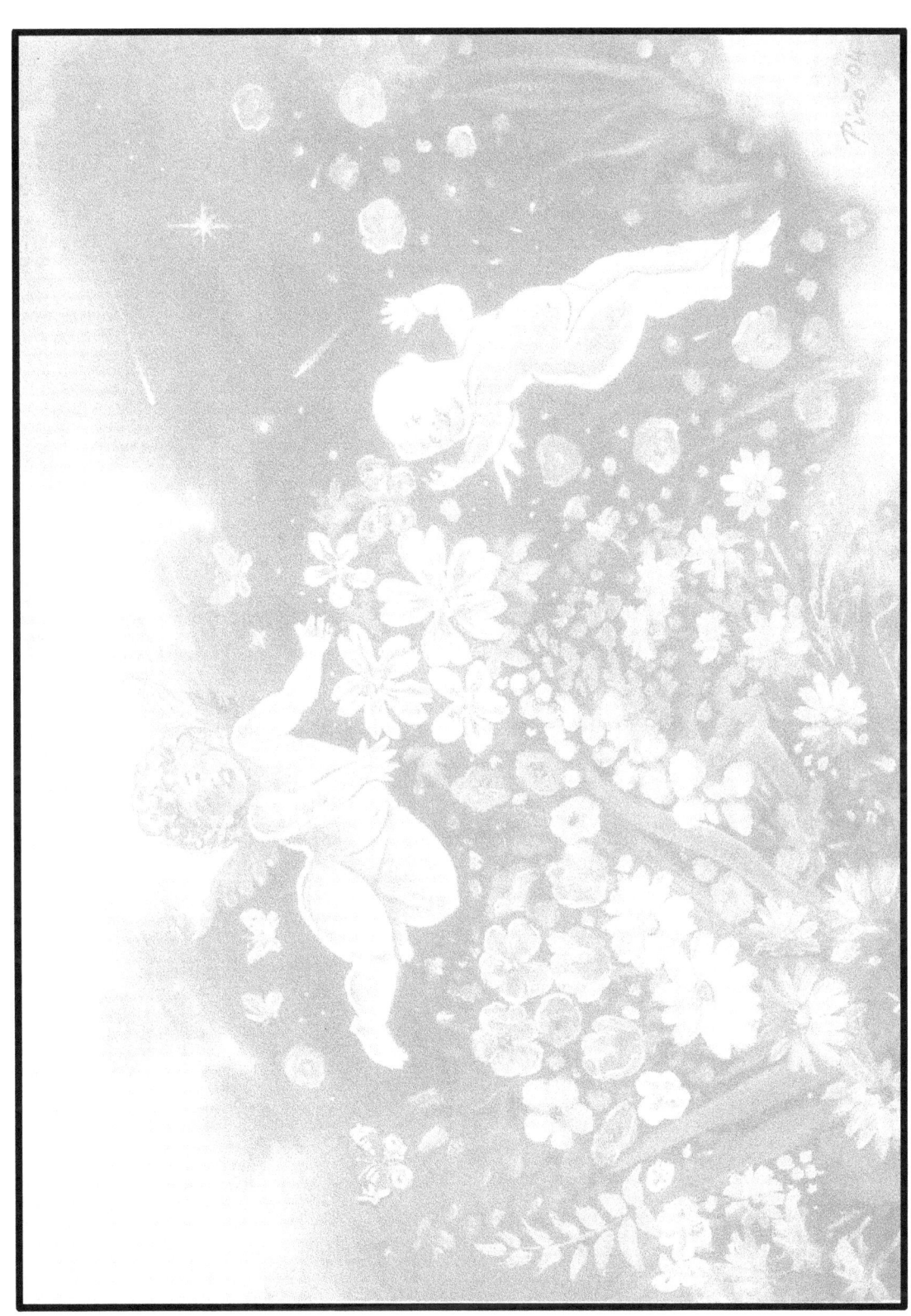

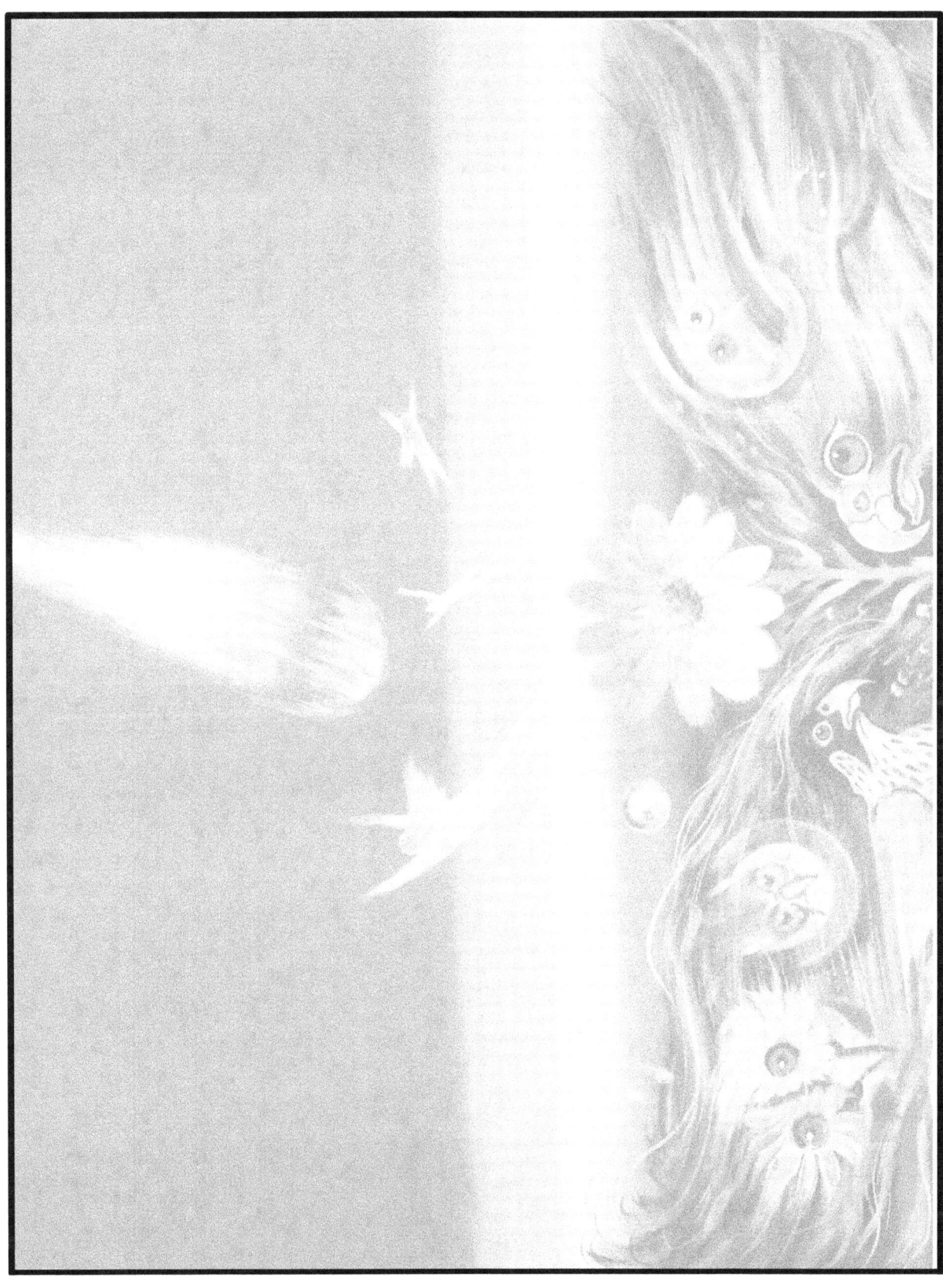

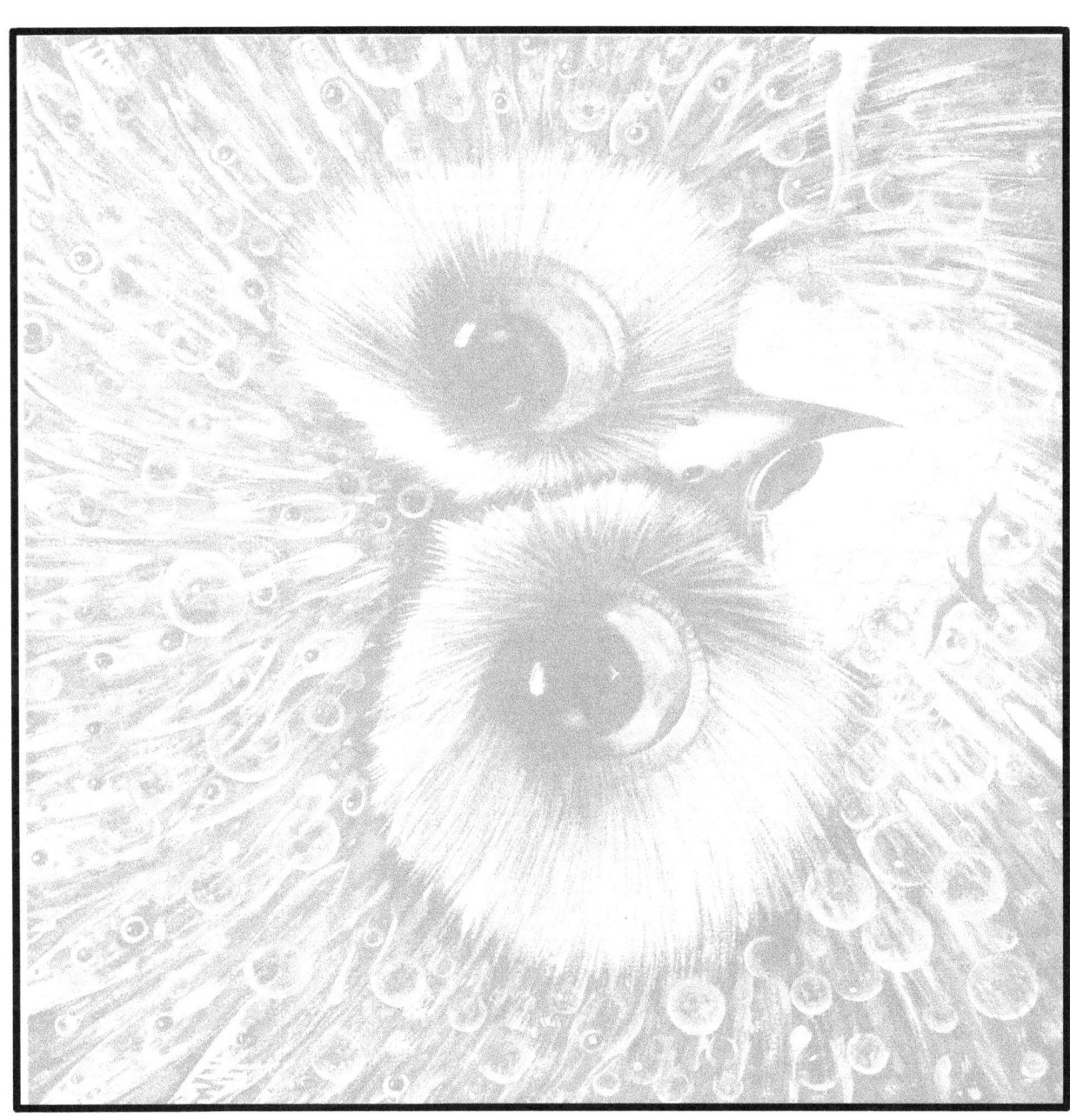

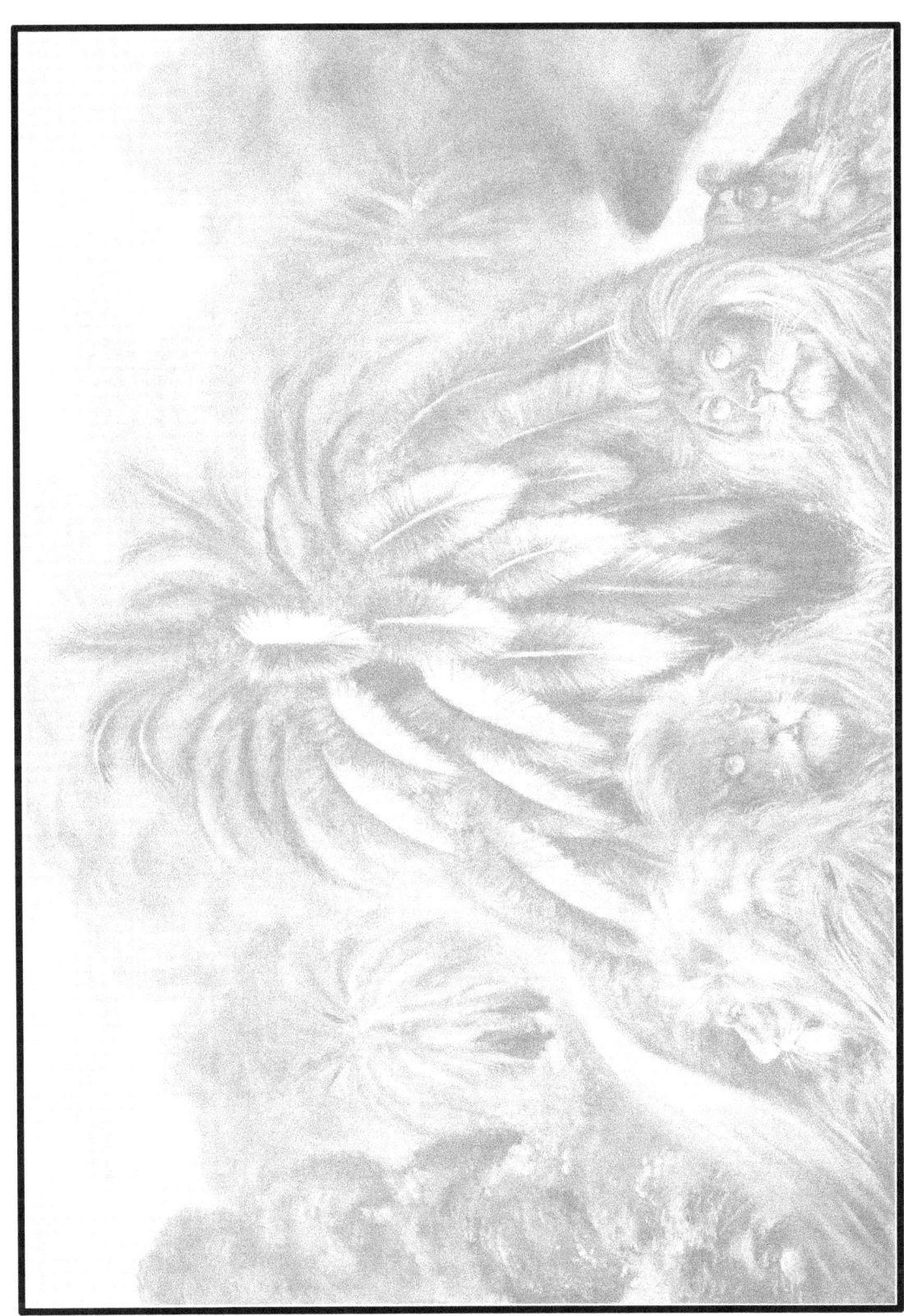

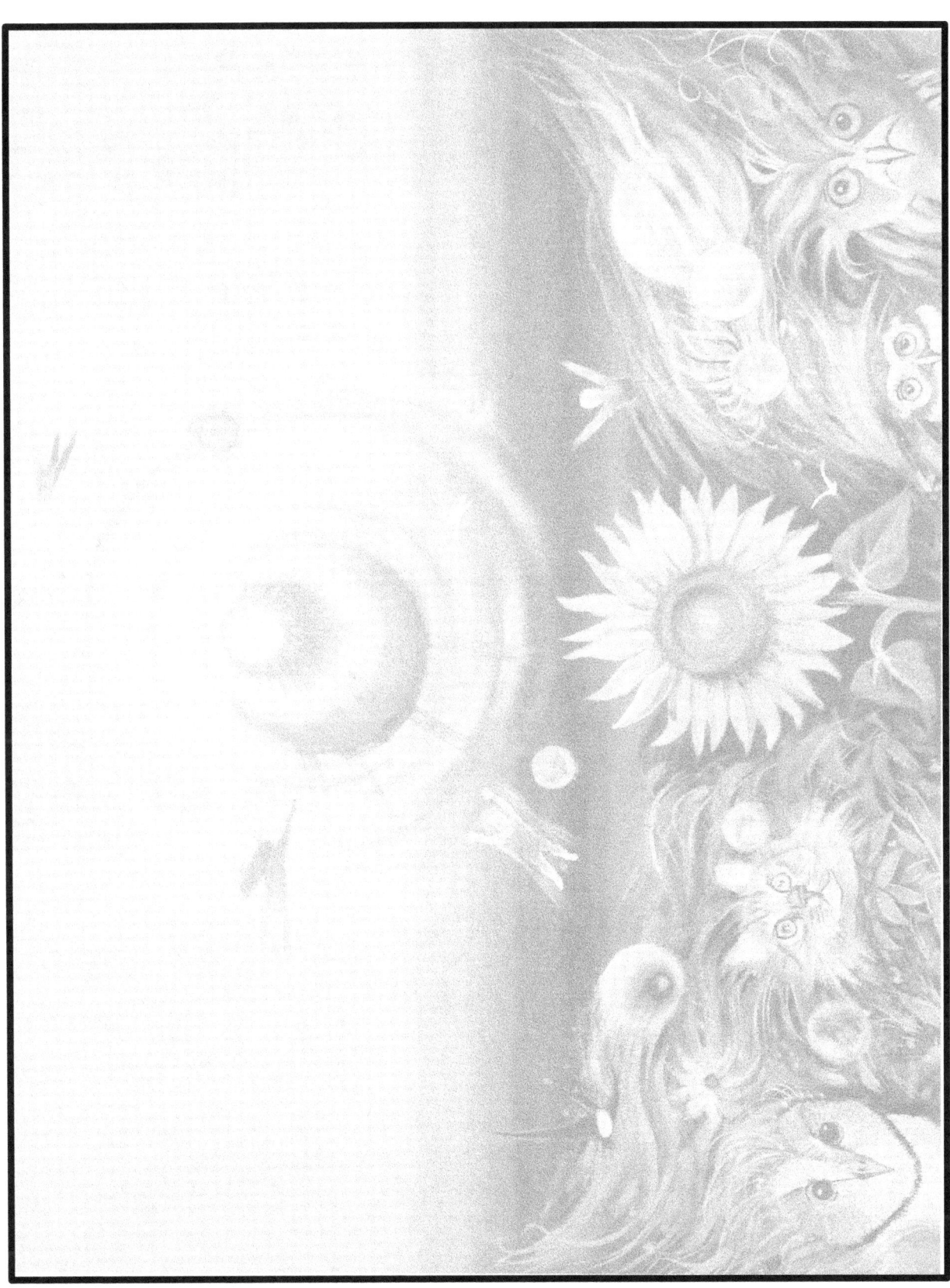

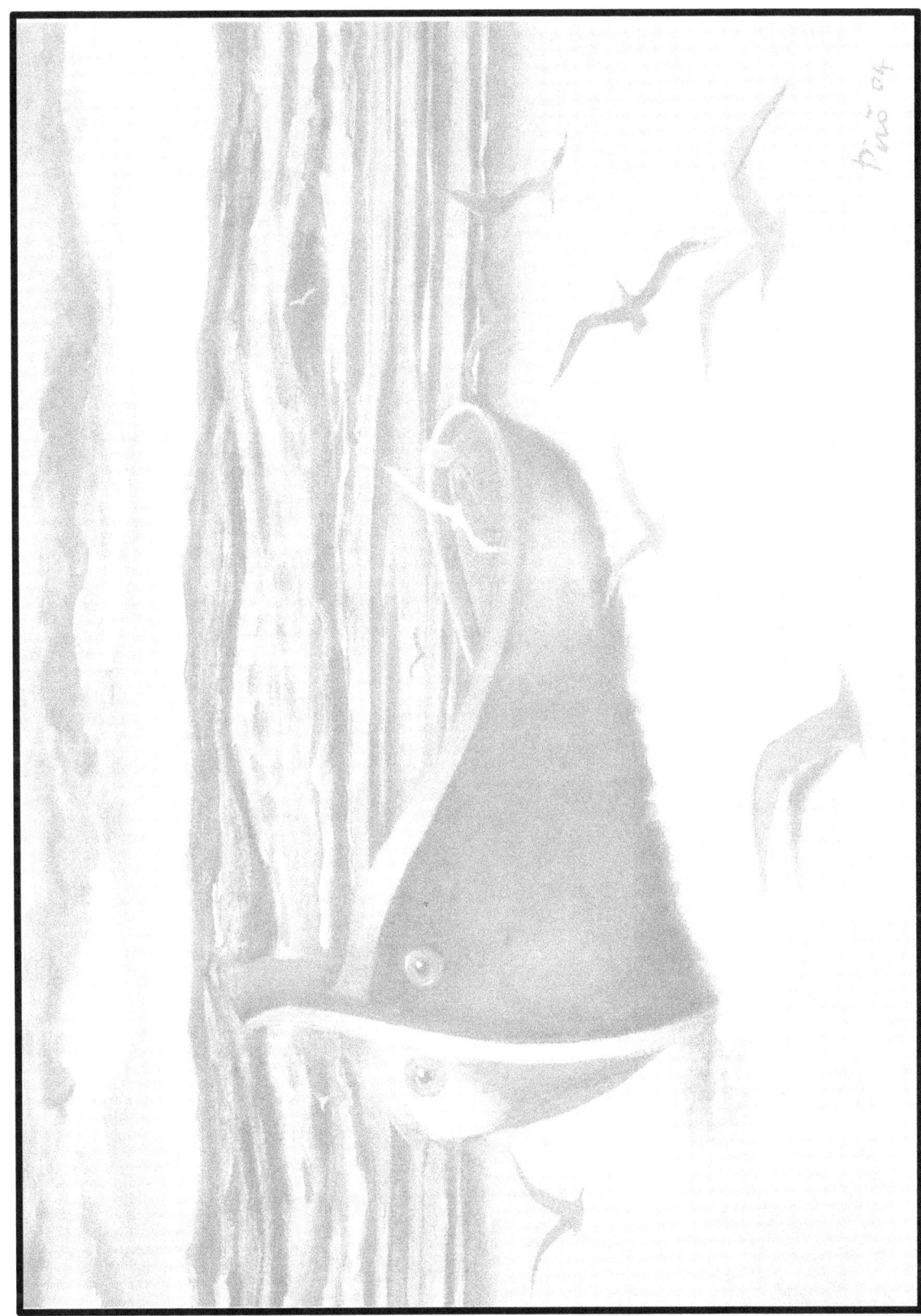

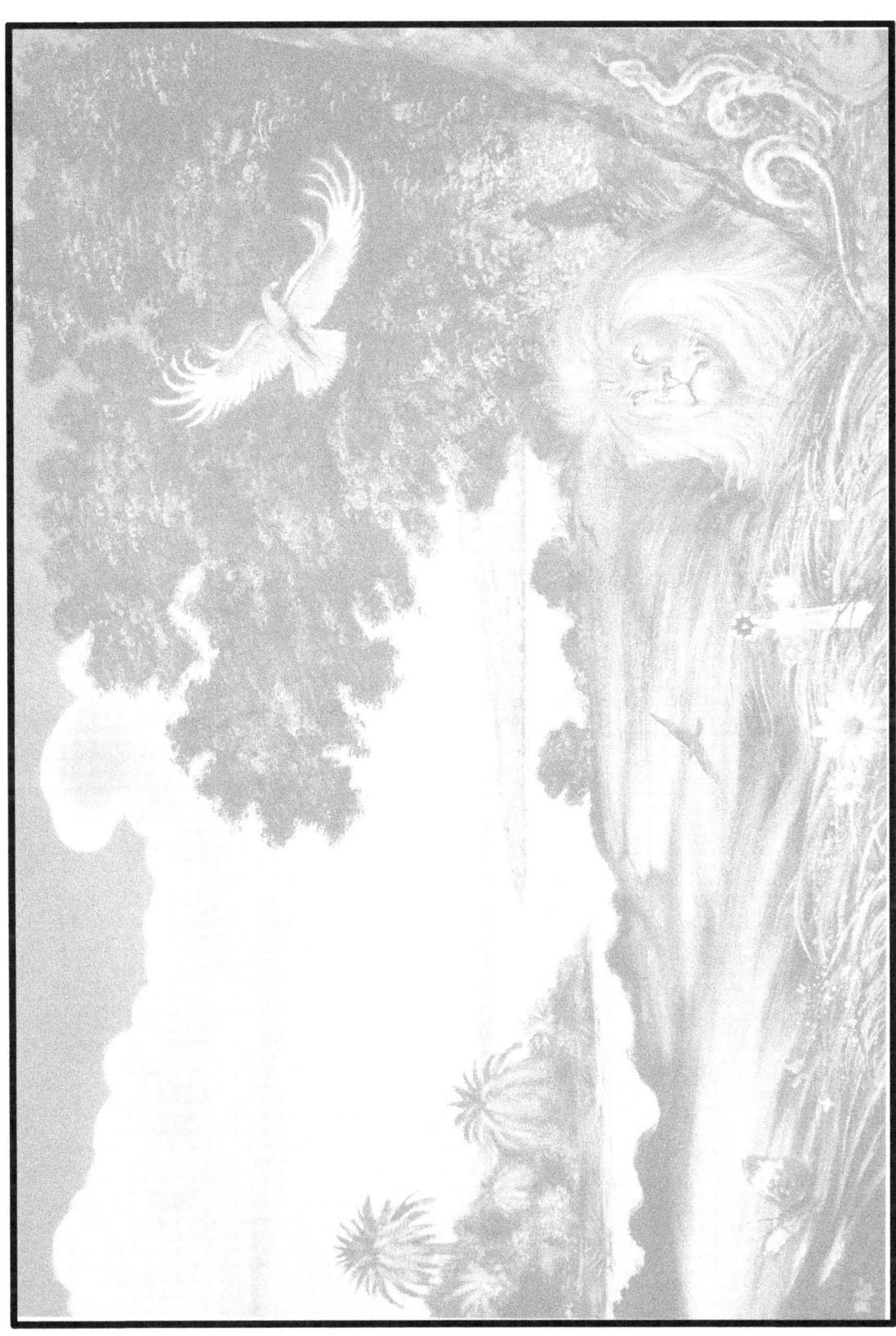

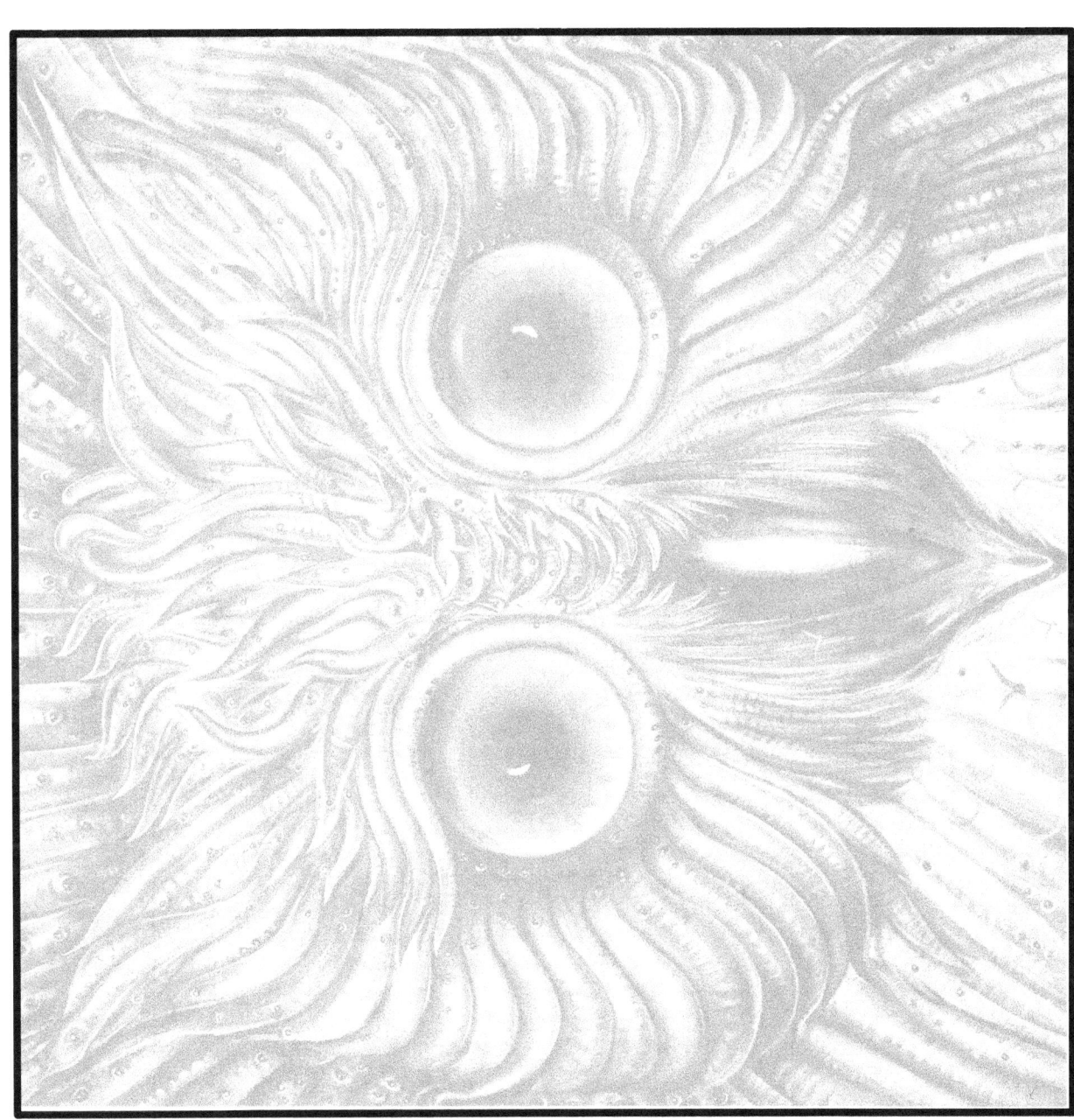

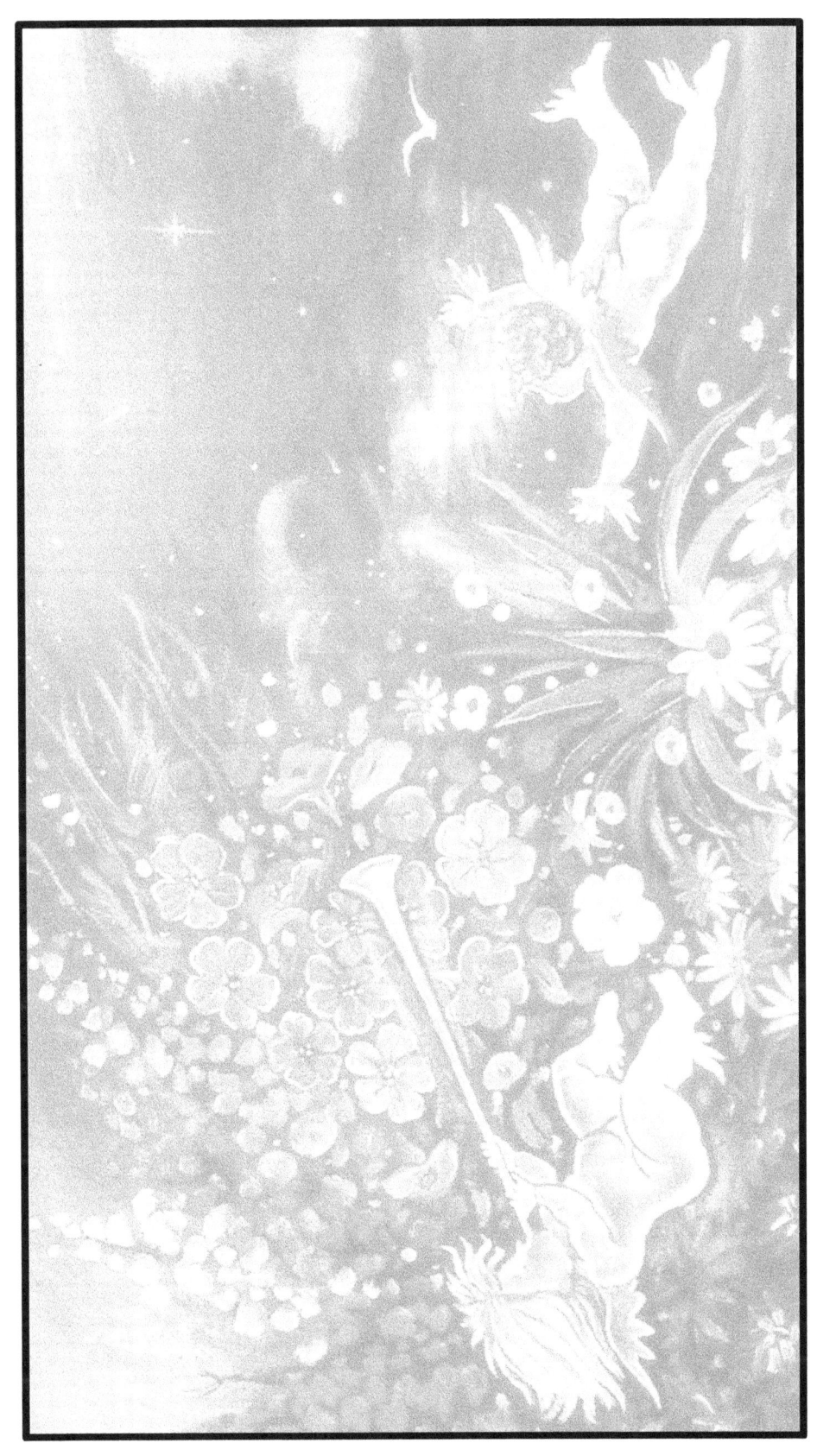

PiRò beside The Royal Peacock

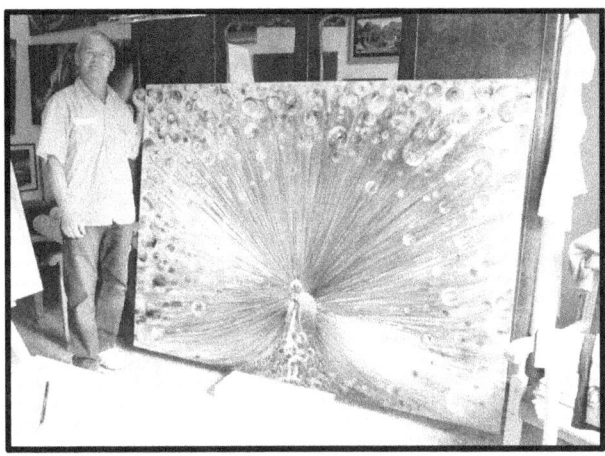

PiRò with Carole Plaxe

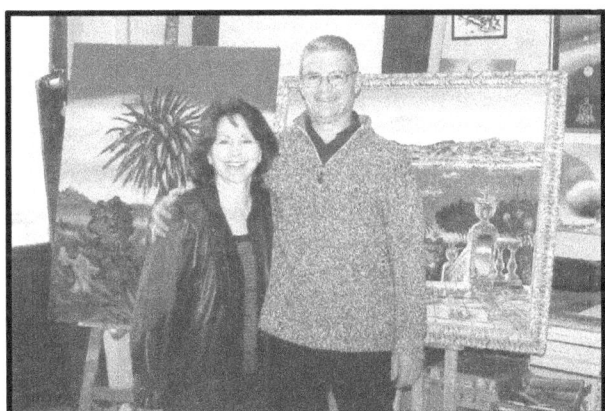

PiRò with Jack Plaxe beside Sincerity

Best buddies!

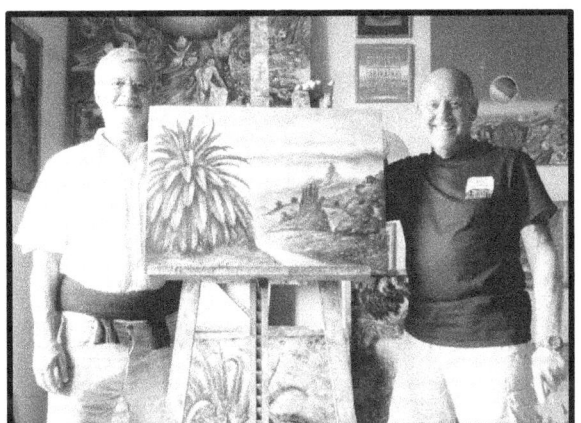
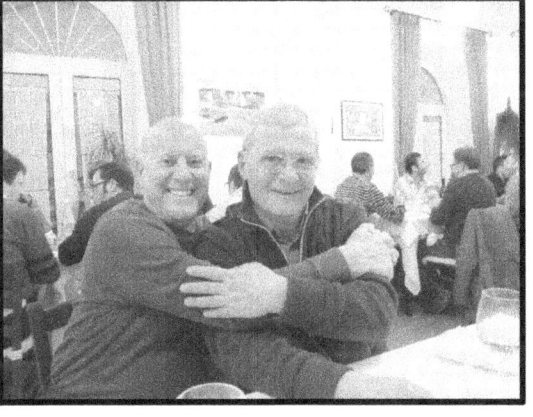

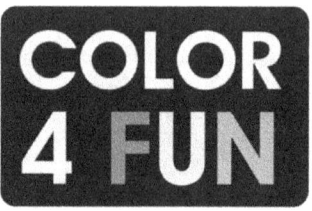

"Mandalas in Grayscale" will be published no later than August 15, 2016. It will contain 20 illustrations such as these:

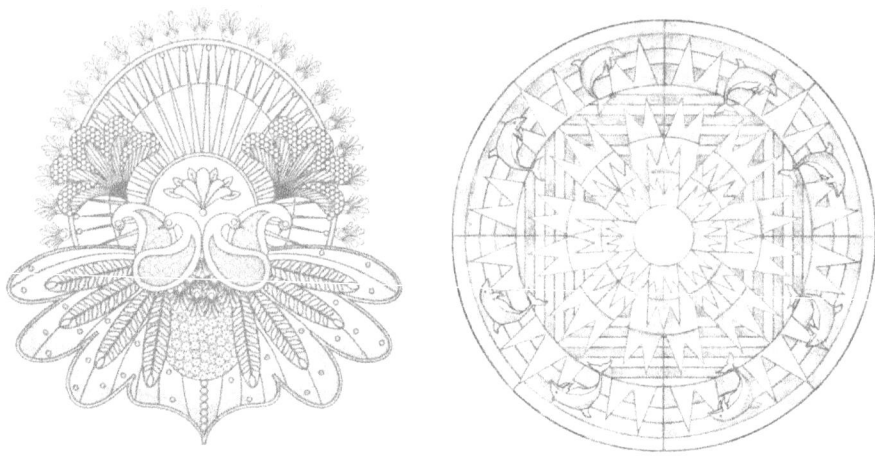

"Italian Fantasy, Volume 2" will be published in September 2016. It will contain 20 grayscale illustrations by the renowned Italian artist Augusta Schinchirimini. Here are two examples from that book:

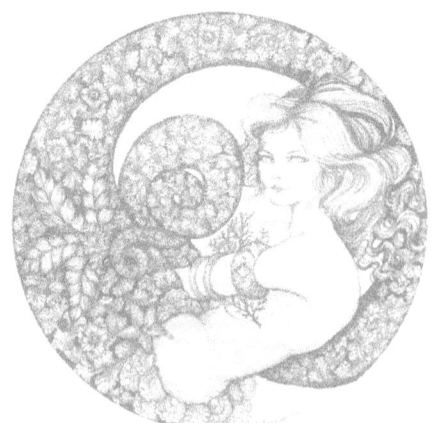
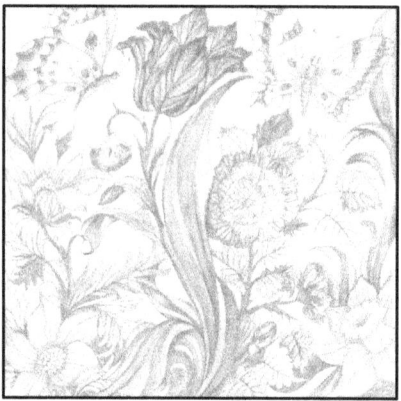

www.ingramcontent.com/pod-product-compliance
Lightning Source LLC
Chambersburg PA
CBHW080138240526

45468CB00009BA/2516